EILEEN GRAY: DESIGNER 1879–1976

J. STEWART JOHNSON

EILEEN GRAY
Designer

Published by Debrett's Peerage Ltd. for
THE MUSEUM OF MODERN ART, NEW YORK

This publication accompanies an exhibition of the work of Eileen
Gray at The Museum of Modern Art, New York. The exhibition
has been made possible by generous support from the Helena
Rubinstein Foundation and The British Council.

First published in the United Kingdom by
Debrett's Peerage Ltd., London, for the Victoria and Albert Museum,
London, and The Museum of Modern Art, New York.

Copyright © Debrett's Peerage Ltd. 1979.
Second printing 1980.

Library of Congress Catalog Card Number 79-66188
Clothbound ISBN 0-87070-307-2
Paperbound ISBN 0-87070-308-0
Book designed by Roger Huggett/Sinc. and printed in England

CONTENTS

Overleaf: Eileen Gray in her nineties.

SOURCES AND ACKNOWLEDGMENTS

The principal source for this book is, or more properly was, Eileen Gray herself, whom I first met in 1971 when she was ninety-two years old. I was in Paris, gathering material for a book that was to compare and contrast the art deco and modernist styles, and went to see her at the suggestion of a friend.

I had no idea what to expect when I approached her flat in the rue Bonaparte and was entirely unprepared for the woman she turned out to be. Thin, straight, dressed in a well-cut blue tweed suit and grey turtle-neck sweater, she wore a dark glass over one eye and was quite deaf. But despite her poor sight and worse hearing (for which she apologized as if it represented a breach of hospitality), I found her to be, on that and subsequent occasions, acute, generous with both her time and knowledge, and a delight-ful companion. She was in the midst of preparing a number of her maquettes of architec-tural projects for shipment to London, as she was donating them to the Royal Institute of British Architects; and my notes of that visit describe her as "very busy, very excited". Though she lacked the stamina of the young, her enthusiasm and interest were extra-ordinarily youthful.

Her memory for the dates of long-past events was not entirely reliable, and over the last years of her life she made repeated attempts to pin them down in chronologies. With the aid of her niece, the English painter Prunella Clough, she sought to set the record straight for the new generation that was taking an interest in her work, most importantly by compiling two large scrapbooks, in which she documented her works with captioned photographs.

These, together with personal conversations, provided the basis for an article on Eileen Gray written by Joseph Rykwert and published in *Domus* in December 1968, and for an exhibition, prepared by Alan Irvine, presented in the Heinz Gallery of the R.I.B.A. in 1971. Both helped bring the designer to the attention of professionals and collectors.

After Eileen Gray's death in 1976, Prunella Clough brought the scrapbooks, chronologies, and all of her other papers to London, and there made them available for this book and the exhibition it is intended to accompany. As she and I went through what at first appeared to be a meagre and haphazard assortment of papers, we discovered that it, in fact, contained biographical material of great value: a day book and lists of customers for Jean Désert, the gallery Eileen Gray maintained from 1922 to 1930; a notebook in her hand with instructions for preparing lacquer; a correspondence with a craftsman named Inagaki, who performed a variety of tasks for her over the years; miscellaneous bills from firms that produced work or supplied materials for her; a group of old press cuttings, indicating critical reaction to her early work; and, finally, a small group of letters she had saved that had been written to her when she was discovered by the Dutch de Stijl architects. I do not mean to suggest that this constituted anything like a full archive; but it was far more than I expected to find and in any event has provided the underpinnings of this book.

The book could not, however, have been written nor the exhibition presented without help that came from many quarters. In Paris, there were Eliane Vinci Leoni-Corradini (who insisted I meet Eileen Gray), Felix Marcilhac, Lynne Thornton, and Mr. and Mrs. Robert Walker; in London, Robin Symes, Christos Michaelides, Philippe Garner, Joseph Rykwert, Monika Kinley, and Erno Goldfinger; and in America, Eyre de Lanux and Sidney and Frances Lewis.

The exhibition was prepared under the auspices of the International Council of The Museum of Modern Art, which I should like to thank for providing the means for an essential trip for research. I should also like to thank the staff of the R.I.B.A. for making available valuable research materials, and Dr. Roy Strong and his staff at the Victoria and Albert Museum, London, for their encouragement with the project.

The New York presentation of the Eileen Gray exhibition was made possible through funding provided by the Helena Rubinstein Foundation and The British Council. I should like to thank them, both personally and on behalf of The Museum of Modern Art, for their generosity.

Finally, I owe two additional debts of gratitude. The first is to Barbara Klein, who managed to convert a particularly rough manuscript into a neat typescript. The last one, and by far the most important, is to Prunella Clough, who in the course of a long and often troubled trans-Atlantic endeavour, has been unfailingly thoughtful, kind, patient, and resourceful. She has become a friend.

J. STEWART JOHNSON
New York
June 19, 1979

EILEEN GRAY: DESIGNER

Eileen Gray in the mid-1920s.

I THE EARLY YEARS

Eileen Gray was born on 9 August 1879, in Brownswood, her family's house, at Enniscorthy, County Wexford, Ireland. The family was Scots-Irish on both sides. Her father, James Maclaren Smith, was an amateur artist who spent much of his time in Europe, painting the scenery of Switzerland and Italy. Her mother was the grand-daughter of the tenth Earl of Moray, and in 1895 she inherited the title Baroness Gray. Two years later Maclaren Smith received a Royal licence to change his name to Smith-Gray, and thereafter the children dropped their father's name and were known simply by the surname Gray.

She grew up the youngest of four children. As a child she occasionally was permitted to travel with her father on the Continent, but most of her time was spent between London, where her mother wintered, and Brownswood. To the end of her long life she remembered with pleasure the plain, rambling Georgian house set on a terraced hill amid well-tended clumps of laurel.

When she was nine her eldest sister married and before long her brother-in-law took over the direction of the family, among other things pulling down the old house and building in its place a much larger one in the Scottish baronial style, which she hated. From then on Brownswood was spoiled for her, and she turned her back on Ireland.

In 1898 she began to study drawing formally at London's Slade School; and it was while there that she learned the technique of making oriental lacquer – not at the Slade but in the shop of D. Charles at 92, Dean Street, which she happened on one day while wandering through Soho, window-shopping during her lunch break from school. Seeing a sign that announced the repair of old lacquer screens, she went upstairs, where the craftsmen showed her what they were doing and explained some of the complicated process of manufacturing lacquer. As she later explained, I was very interested, because I'd always wanted to learn lacquer; and so I said, "I suppose I could never come here and work", and they said, "But you can – of course you can. Start Monday if you like". And so I started and for years I was friends with them.[1] Thus, casually, almost by accident, Eileen Gray began the work that would provide the focus for her career through the next twenty-five years.

Her father had not been well for some time – in fact, at one point, after he had had an early stroke, the entire family had gone to Switzerland to look after him – and in 1900 he died. By 1902 Eileen Gray had decided to try to fashion a life for herself in Paris.

At first her time was filled with drawing classes, initially at the Académie Colarossi and then at the Académie Julien; with continuing her efforts to gain a mastery of oriental lacquer, and with finding an apartment into which she could settle and which would make it possible for her to put down roots. Before she could do this, however, in 1905,

The 'Le Destin' screen.

she contracted typhoid fever, a case so severe that she was not expected to survive. She recovered, however, and during her convalescence went to Algeria, where she no doubt first saw the flat-roofed, white houses that were to influence so many of the young modernists.

In 1907 she found an apartment at 21, rue Bonaparte, in an eighteenth-century hotel a block from the Seine, which she would keep throughout the rest of her life. By this time she had also met and begun to work with Sugawara, a Japanese master of lacquer; and with him she continued to explore the many subtleties of this demanding medium.

Oriental lacquer is made by building up numerous thin layers of a resin (obtained from the *Rhus Vernicifera*, a tree in the acacia family), which when hardened forms a lustrous surface that is impermeable to water. The process by which lacquer is made is extraordinarily demanding, requiring both patience and diligence – patience because each layer must be allowed three days in a humid room to harden before the next can be applied; diligence not the least because the resin is noxious and lacquer workers are subject to painful rashes.

At least twenty-two steps are required in making lacquer. First a thin coat of natural lacquer is applied to a smooth surface of wood. When this has dried, a second coat mixed with a fine earth imported from Japan is added in order to fill in any cracks in the wood; and onto this is laid a piece of stretched cloth, the purpose of which is to form a uniform base for subsequent coats of lacquer and to cushion any shocks or breaks that might damage the finished surface and permit the infiltration of water. From this point onward, as far as the artist is concerned, the object becomes lacquer, the wooden core having disappeared. Upon this base eight coats of lacquer and Japanese earth are added, each of which, when hardened, is carefully pumiced to make it absolutely smooth and unblemished. An eleventh coat of pure natural lacquer, is applied to stabilize the layers beneath it. Then six more coats of lacquer mixed with extremely fine Japanese earth are added. The eighteenth coat is the first into which pigment is introduced, and it is followed by two more coats, each of which is meticulously pumiced. Finally, several coats may be added introducing applied decoration (including such foreign materials as gold or silver leaf, bits of eggshell, or mother-of-pearl).

Eileen Gray practiced this painstaking technique first with the workmen at D. Charles in Soho and then with Sugawara, who would work for her well into the 'twenties. Gradually she filled a notebook with recipes for achieving different colours and surface textures in lacquer. It is not known when she moved from being a student, an amateur, to becoming a professional; but by 1913 she was confident enough to exhibit examples of her work in the *Salon de la Société des Artistes Décorateurs*[2] and had achieved a mastery of the medium which recommended her to one of the most discerning patrons of the day, the *grand couturier* Jacques Doucet.

Jacques Doucet was famous not only as a leader of fashion but as a collector and connoisseur of art[3]. Until 1912 he had concentrated on works of the eighteenth century, but in June of that year he sold his drawings, pastels, sculpture, paintings, furniture, and objets d'art, as well as the house he had built to hold them. The auction of his collection took four days and realized 13,884,360 francs (about 4,000,000 old francs), most of which he subsequently used to finance a library on the history of art that, by the time he presented it to the nation in 1918, included 100,000 volumes, 15,000 manuscripts, and

Round table owned by Jacques Doucet.

150,000 photographs. In 1912 he also took a new apartment in Neuilly in which he hung paintings by Manet, Degas, Van Gogh, and Cézanne, and began to collect works by Matisse, Picasso, and Brancusi, and examples of African sculpture. Now, also, he began to replace the furnishings made by the great ébénistes of the eighteenth century that had filled his earlier house with the work of some of the most original designers of his own time: Pierre Legrain, Paul Iribe, Marcel Coard, and Eileen Gray.

Eileen Gray made at least two tables for Doucet[4]. One, a high, long table in dark green lacquer, has legs carved to represent clusters of lotus flowers, the stylized blossoms of which are white. Its top extends at either end to form rings, through which are threaded long, green silk ropes terminating in amber balls and silk tassels. The effect is precious, exotic, theatrical. The other, at first glance more conventional, is actually the more original and exhibits marked affinities to the designer's later, more architectural work. It is a low, two-tiered round table supported on four short legs. The black lacquer shelf and top are unornamented, save for the representation of a red and silver cup and ball near the edge of the top[5]. But it is the legs which give the table its distinction. They appear to be built up out of neat stacks of cubical and rectangular blocks made of dull, mottled silver lacquer. The lowest blocks support the shelf, which in turn forms a base for the stacked blocks above it. Each pile of blocks is arranged to form long open slits within it, and the play of solids and voids that results from this piercing lightens the piece and gives it tension. We cannot be certain when these tables were made[6], but Doucet also acquired from Eileen Gray the only known signed and dated example of her work – the so-called 'Le Destin' screen.

This four-panel screen, signed by the artist and dated 1914 is made of deep red lacquer. The front portrays two nude youths in blue-black. The first strides forward, burdened by the enormous silver-grey apparition of a shrouded old man; the second, only partially revealed at the extreme right of the screen, as if entering unexpectedly, recoils in horror at the real and symbolic figures before him. No attempt is made to provide a setting for the scene; there is not even any indication of the ground on which they walk or of a horizon, and yet the figures seem rooted in real space. The effect is at once highly dramatic and elegantly decorative. In fact, so stylish is the front of the screen that one is completely unprepared for its back. Here, the same dull red serves as a background for a totally abstract design of swirling lines and planes, in tarnished silvery greys. No attempt is made to suggest depth on either the front or back of the screen; both compositions are explicitly two-dimensional. And yet the contrast between the chic figurative tableau on the front and the uncompromising abstraction on the back is startling. The screen is a *tour-de-force*. It is as if the artist, confident of her skill and imagination, were proclaiming her ability to move with equal ease in any direction she chose – either towards the sophisticated decoration espoused by such artists as Léon Bakst, Paul Iribe, and Georges Lepape, or towards rigorous modernism.

In time, Eileen Gray would entirely forsake the decorative, but for the next ten years most of her work retained some connection with conventional representation. With the coming of the 1914 war, she drove an ambulance in Paris for a time and then returned to London to wait out the war, taking Sugawara with her and setting up a studio near Cheyne Walk in which she could continue her work.

In 1917, the English edition of *Vogue* published an effusive article on her[7], which illustrated, in addition to Doucet's screen, four new designs: a four-panel screen in blue lacquer encrusted with mother-of-pearl depicting a running figure seemingly pursued by a stream of tiny stars; a panel for a door with transported figures, hands thrust forward, heads thrown back; a 'sand-grey table top, where white fishes dart about a black pool, in which float strange, grey leaf-forms'[8]; and a design for a table top, 'which dimly suggests the zodiac . . . palely illumined by a silver planet'. All, while retaining some connection to conventional representational art, are far more enigmatic than the 'Le Destin' screen. The viewer must search for the subject within them, and in the case of the zodiac design, the only element that is at all literal is the little planet.

NOTES

1. Aquarius interview, videotaped.
2. A panel showing three antique figures, the centre one nude and holding a lotus blossom, is illustrated in *Art et Décoration*, March 1913, p. 91.
3. For further information of Doucet see J. F. Revel, "Jacques Doucet, Couturier et Collectionneur", *L'OEil*, December 1961, pp. 44–51, and André Joubin, "Jacques Doucet, 1853–1929", *Gazette des Beaux Arts*, March 1930, pp. 69–82.
4. The sale of objects from the Doucet Collection at the Hotel Drouot (8 November 1972), included also a third table, lot 35, which was listed as being "anonymous" but may also have been designed by Eileen Gray, who, according to a note to the author from Lynne Thornton, on seeing it recalled having designed its carved rams-head brackets but could not remember making the entire table.
5. Prunella Clough wrote the author at the time of the Doucet sale that this decoration was not by Eileen Gray.
6. The repetition of the lotus motif used by the artist in the panel she exhibited in 1913 suggests a similar date for the large table.
7. A.S., "An Artist in Lacquer", *Vogue* (Early August 1917), p. 29.
8. She would use this pattern also in a rug she named "Poissons".

II RUE DE LOTA

After the Armistice, Eileen Gray returned to Paris with Sugawara and reopened her workshops. By March 1919 she had begun to create a decorative scheme for the rue de Lota apartment of Madame Mathieu Lévy, who under the name Suzanne Talbot was one of the most successful modistes in Paris. This job, which eventually involved the design and execution of furniture, carpets, lighting fixtures, and entire new walls of lacquer was to be the most ambitious commission for decoration of Eileen Gray's career and marked a further step away from her early decorative manner, with its affinities to the developing French art deco style, to her later, more architectural approach to design.

Among the furniture she designed for Madame Lévy were two pieces of remarkable theatricality. One was a low, arch-backed armchair upholstered in salmon silk, the front legs of which, sweeping upward in continuous curves to become arms, were carved and finished in salmon-yellow lacquer to resemble rearing serpents. The other was a chaise longue in patinated brown lacquer, shaped like a graceful pirogue and supported on a base of twelve shallow arches. Had Eileen Gray continued to design in this vein, her work would no doubt have become known as bizarre, luxurious, and eccentric. Such qualities were in vogue. But already she was tending toward a different sort of design, no less personal but much more restrained.

A long, low, bookcase she designed for the apartment, for example, was very much at odds with prevailing taste. *Bibliothèques*, a popular form, were generally conceived of as tall, massive closed cupboards, their monumentality sometimes being emphasized by placing them on platforms. Eileen Gray's bookcase, only three shelves high, was open, and the strong horizontals of the frame and exposed shelves were further accentuated with repeated horizontal incised lines picked out in a buff lacquer to contrast with the dark brown background of the piece.

Even more indicative of the direction in which she was tending was her treatment of the apartment's walls, which she described as having "disgraceful mouldings" when she found them[1]. These she hid completely – in the bedroom with floor-to-ceiling hand-woven hangings having an overall pattern of thin horizontal lines; in the salon by encasing the old walls with large lacquer panels butted together and decorated with abstract designs similar to those she had used on the back of the 'Le Destin' screen. The recently finished salon was illustrated in the September 1920 issue of *Harper's Bazaar*, which observed that:

> the walls might pose as studies from the latest Cubist exhibition. At least
> one panel might be "The Nude Descending the Staircase" but, in fact, the design
> is achieved by streaking the black lacquer with over-tones of silver, slightly

tarnished in places. And because of the softness of the silver tones, the effect is really both interesting and peaceful . . . Of course, one might imagine that the owner of a salon with a framework so apparently sombre would choose brilliant colours for the furnishings. Not this owner nor this artist. The carpet is black and of a most luxurious depth and softness, . . . the desk is a soft mellow black and so are most of the chairs[2].

It was not the salon, however, that was the most strikingly innovative aspect of the apartment, but the manner in which she treated the walls of the gallery leading to Madame Lévy's bedroom. This space apparently was not transformed until the summer of 1922, for on 23 May of that year Eileen Gray received a letter from Inagaki, a craftsman to whom she farmed out a variety of work over the years (carving, ivory handles, lacquering, etc.) in which he explained that his estimate for the screen, about which they had obviously had earlier discussions, was contingent on his taking three months to execute it, and that if she insisted on his doing the work faster he would have to raise enormously the price he had quoted her. He then went on to assure her that if she permitted him to begin in a month and take the full three months, the price would be: "1 paravent: 450 pièces à 8f50 pièce soit 3,825f. Bois fourni par vous."

This screen composed of 450 pieces can only have been the one with which Eileen Gray lined the walls of Madame Lévy's gallery; for although after that date she was to adapt her basic design to several different uses, she would never again have an occasion to build so large a screen.

Right: Suzanne Talbot (Mme. Mathieu Lévy) reclining in her chaise longue. Behind her is a panelled wall of the salon.

The chaise longue made for the rue de Lota apartment.

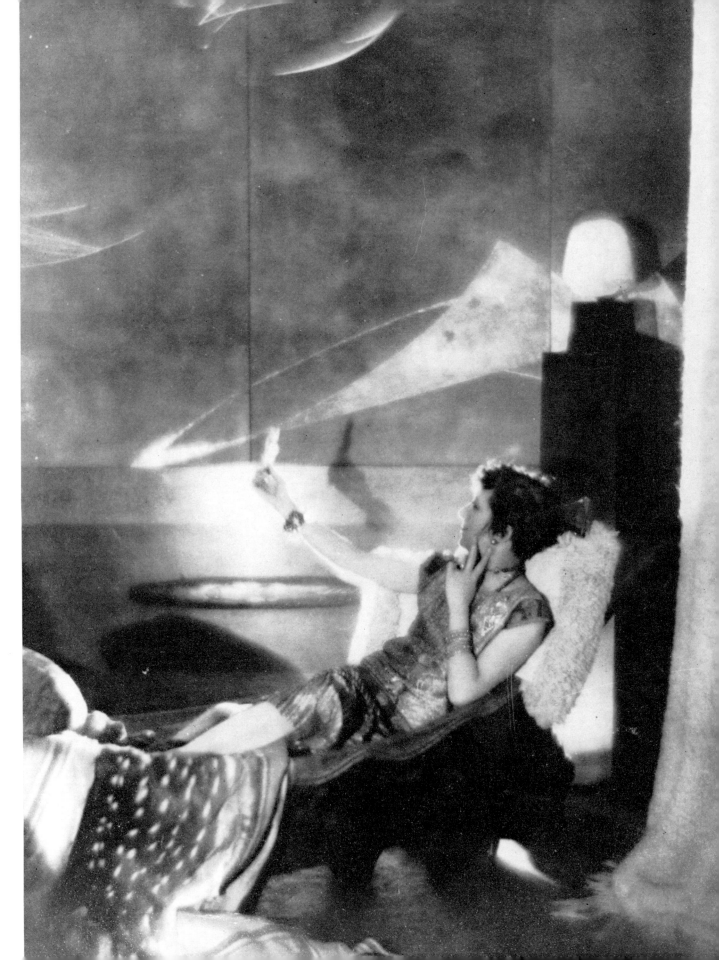

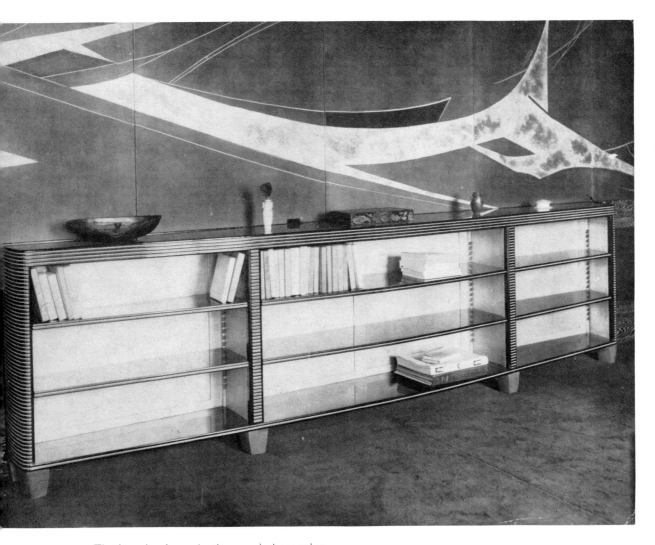

The long bookcase in the rue de Lota salon.

Her idea here was to substitute for the large panels used in the salon entire new walls built up out of thin lacquer plaques. It was as if she were laying brick walls, the bricks made of lacquer textured with powdered stone but otherwise undecorated, the only pattern – but of course that a very strong one – being the staggered outlines of the bricks themselves. The gallery was relatively long and narrow, and in order both to give the illusion of its being shorter and to give added importance to the double door centred on the far wall, which opened into Madame Lévy's bedroom, she created a little vestibule by turning the bricks inward on either side before the end of the gallery and piercing the screen so that one glimpsed the space beyond it. The means are simple, the effect unexpected and exciting.

NOTES

1. Eileen Gray typewritten caption accompanying a photograph of the rue de Lota apartment, in one of the scrapbooks
2. Unsigned article, "Lacquer Walls and Furniture Displace Old Gods in Paris and London", *Harper's Bazaar*, September 1920.

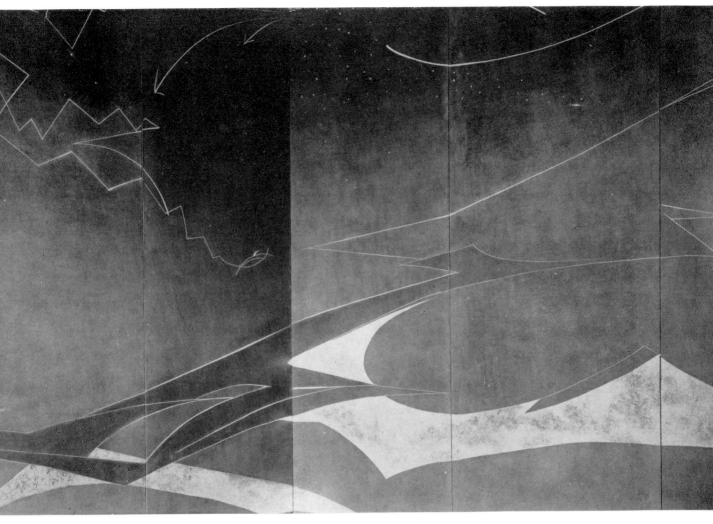

A corner of the salon. The design continues between panels and around the corner without interruption.

Overleaf: The gallery leading to Mme. Mathieu Lévy's bedroom. The lacquer "bricks" encase the original walls.

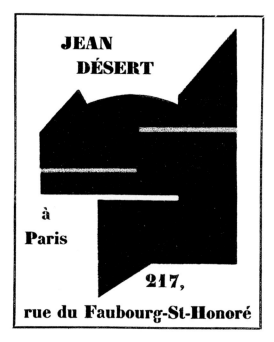

JEAN
DÉSERT

à
Paris

217,
rue du Faubourg-St-Honoré

Right: Chest-of-drawers made for Jean Désert. Eileen Gray's recipe book gives directions for distressing wood to give it the appearance of an ancient sarcophagus. The handles are made of bone.

Cover of an announcement for Jean Désert.

In the late spring of 1922, in addition to carrying the work at the rue de Lota into its final stage, Eileen Gray opened a gallery in which she could exhibit and sell her designs. It was located at 217, rue du Faubourg-St. Honoré, opposite the Salle Pleyel, and was called "Jean Désert". How she chose the name is not known; there was no such person. In the gallery she showed examples from all her areas of design: lacquer screens, both lacquer and wooden furniture, lamps, divans, mirrors, and hand-woven hangings and carpets. The gallery's card also offered "Décoration et Installation d'Apartements". From time to time she would exhibit along with her own things the work of other artists. She showed sculptures by Osip Zadkine, for example, and in 1923 wood engravings by Chana Orloff. Essentially, however, Jean Désert was a showplace for her own designs, which she found it economical to produce in small series of four or five.

Although her principal interest was in designing objects to be made in lacquer, for some time she had also been designing carpets. About 1910 she took an apartment in the rue Visconti, which she used as a studio for the making of carpets. She and the English artist Evelyn Wyld purchased looms in England and brought over a weaver to teach a group of apprentices they hired how to operate them. Eileen Gray provided designs for the studio, which Evelyn Wyld ran.

Large cabinet in sycomore designed for the architect Henri Pacon, probably about 1926. Some of the drawers pivot, a device first seen in a coiffeuse Eileen Gray exhibited in the 1923 Salon and one she used on several later occasions.

Rug with abstract design made for Jean Désert.

Hanging lantern exhibited above the couch in the bedroom-boudoir for Monte Carlo. The sides are deep blue glass, the triangular shapes rough-textured silver.

From the start, there was a much greater demand for Eileen Gray's carpets than for the lacquer objects, which, of course, were far more expensive. Throughout the year 1923, for instance, Jean Désert's daybook notes sales of twenty-one carpets of various designs, while there are only three large pieces of furniture listed: an armchair, "Sirène", in black lacquer, a red lacquer desk, and a coiffeuse (bought by the Vicomte Charles de Noailles). In addition to these, she sold two lamps, two lanterns, two parchment lampshades, a lacquer hand mirror, a hanging, four cushions, six furs (which were fashionable for use either as rugs or as throws to cover furniture), and a Zebra skin. The price of the Zebra skin, by the way, at 3,800 francs, far exceeded those of the furniture; the armchair cost 1,000 francs, the desk 1,200, and the coiffeuse 1,600.

Although in this year Eileen Gray made a considerable effort – an effort which, as we shall see, may have done the gallery more harm than good – to achieve wide recognition by creating an ambitious display of her work for the Salon des Artistes Décorateurs, 1923's sales are not dissimilar to those of other years. Her output was small; but her clientele, though obviously very limited, was international, including not only French but also American, British, and Belgian collectors. During this period she maintained not only the Faubourg-St. Honoré gallery, but also a workshop devoted mostly to furniture and lacquer at 11, rue Guènégaud (the letterhead of which was "Désert et Gray" and which may have functioned as well as a boutique) and the thriving carpet workshop in the rue Visconti under the direction of Evelyn Wyld.

Lacquer screen bearing a geometric linear design.

Eight-panel lacquer screen.

In 1927 Evelyn Wyld left Eileen Gray and began to design as well as make carpets, subsequently collaborating in a new venture with Eyre de Lanux, a younger American painter who was responsible for designing the new firm's furniture and decorative schemes. Unfortunately, Jean Désert's accounts exist only through 1927, and so it is impossible to assess the full effect of Evelyn Wyld's loss to the business. Eileen Gray does appear to have attempted to have carpets made outside, for there exists a letter to "Monsieur Jean Désert" dated 14 December 1928 from Emile Chaumeron "Manufacture de Tapis et Tissus Végétaux" giving an estimate of 516.90 francs for making a plain carpet with bands of white and chestnut-coloured wool. But by this time she had largely lost interest in the gallery, most of her attention having turned to architecture.

Early in 1930 she closed down Jean Désert, after having reduced the prices on a number of remaining pieces of furniture in order to sell them off quickly. Two lists exist of furniture "à la boutique" at that time, the second, with minor variations in descriptions, headed "Derniers prix des meubles".

This inventory, (below) – the only one known ever to have been made of the stock of Jean Désert – suggests that many of the objects on hand had been designed and probably made many years earlier. The water-lily (nénuphar) table suggests her commissions for Jacques Doucet. The Persian bed and boat-shaped bed sound like the sort of furniture she had made for the rue de Lota apartment almost ten years before. The blue glass lantern had been exhibited in 1923. By 1930, such objects, which had represented very advanced style when they were originally conceived, had come to seem dated. Popular taste was swinging towards a more austere, less decorated kind of design. For Eileen Gray, the swing had been made years earlier and the closing of Jean Désert was little more than a formal acknowledgment of this fact.

LISTS DES MEUBLES (À LA BOUTIQUE)[1]

1 Grande table laque marron	13,500	9,500
*1 d° noire decoupée	11,000	7,400
*1 Bibliothèque	13,500	
1 Table ronde	1,700	
*1 Table à thé	2,000	
1 [petite] Table à tiroirs	1,500	1,300
1 Coiffeuse [chène]	1,400	1,150
[1 Coiffeuse avec tiroirs]	[1,800]	
2 Tables poirier à 500f	1,000	
1 Bureau	10,800	7,800
1 Table nénuphar	8,000	4,300
1 Table ovale rouge	8,000	4,800
2 Socles noirs à 400f	800	
1 d° d° sycomore	350	
1 Lit de repos laque nois [AD][2]	8,000	6,800
1 Lit bateau	14,000	9,800
1 Lit Persan	6,500	Recouvert
1 Divan bas bois brûlé	2,300	2,100
1 d° satin noir (avec coussins)	1,250	quel est ce meuble?
1 Paravent lignes	17,000	13,500
*1 d° sabi d'argent	11,000	8,500
1 d° noir et argent	11,000	9,000
1 Petit paravent blanc [et écaille]	10,000	5,200
1 d° d° marron	9,500	7,200

2 Paravents briques à 800f	1,600	
1 d° décor sur toile noir	7,800	5,200
1 Panneaux sur toile rouge et blanc	4,000	
1 Glace rouge	2,000	1,800
1 d° marron [et argent]	2,000	1,600
1 Grande glace	3,000	2,200
1 Glace escalier	2,000	1,650
3 Glaces à mains laqué à 260f	780	
2 d° chêne à 125f	250	
1 peau de Zèbre	2,500	
1 d° chèvre	95	
*1 d° mouton blanc	100	
3 Petites peaux de ? à 75f	225	
*1 Mouton marron		
2 Léopards à 700	1,400	
1 rideau bourrette soie		
1 Dessus lit rouge	2,200	
1 paire Rideaux à franges à 800	1,600	
(2 Tentures ou rideaux sans prix) pas en rente		
2 Lampes lanternes colle de peau à 250f	500	
7 d° en laque à 700³	4,900	
1 avec petits motifs d'ivoire	800	
2 avec anneaux d'ivoire à 950f⁴	1,900	
1 Lampe Cubiste	1,600	
1 Lanterne verre bleu	575	
2 appliques, ébène maccassar (les 2)	540	340
4 d° or et argent à 280f	1,120	
1 Lampe à fleurs	950	
2 Lampes escaliers à 700f	1,400	
1 (petit paravent projet)		
1 petit panneau laque [jaune]	2,000	
[1 Divan coffres marron]	[11,000]	
[1 pouf]	[1,800]	
	———	
	211,935	
	———	

NOTES

1. Those items marked with an * have blue pencil lines drawn through them and presumably were sold between the making of the first and second lists. Brackets indicate additional information found on the second list.
2. Presumably this is the bed she exhibited in her bedroom-boudoir in the 1923 Salon des Artistes Décorateurs.
3. The second list breaks this down into:
   1 Lanterne oeuf d'autriche (peinte rouge) 200
   6 d° d° laqués et decoupees.
4. On the second list, this becomes:
   1 Lanterne peinte en blanc avec ceinture de laque noir
   1 d° avec anneaux d'ivoire 500

Black block screen. One of several variations made for
Jean Désert from a design developed in 1923.

The "bedroom-boudoir for Monte Carlo", exhibited in the fourteenth Salon des Artistes Décorateurs. Severely criticized in the French press, it was much admired by J. J. P. Oud.

Black lacquer desk and red and black bench, exhibited in the 1923 Salon. The ivory handles may have been carved by Inagaki, who carved many such handles for Eileen Gray. Their surviving correspondence, which begins in 1918 and runs through 1922 reveals that she would supply him with models for the ivory handles she wanted, which she would make out of either wax or potatoes.

1923 was a crucial year for Eileen Gray. Jean Désert had been open long enough to have gained a considerable amount of favourable notice from the press not only in Paris but in London and New York – and to have attracted a small but influential clientele. Her designs were rapidly evolving, away from the highly decorative art deco style[1] and towards a more formal and austere expression. In order to draw attention to her new work, she prepared for the Salon des Artistes Décorateurs (in which she had last exhibited ten years earlier) an ambitious display, which she entitled a "room-boudoir for Monte Carlo".

The scheme was focused on a divan of zebra wood piled with cushions, which stood before panels lacquered with an abstract design in matt white and red. This was flanked by two of her pierced screens – developed from the "bricks" she had first used in the gallery of Suzanne Talbot's rue de Lota apartment. To one side was a raised entry with a door lacquered in very dark brown and dull gold. The carpet was dark blue and brown with an abstract design in pale grey. A hanging lantern in blue glass and silver hung above the couch; and other examples of her furniture and lighting fixtures were disposed within the area.

If she had expected this room, which bore virtually no resemblance to the conventional model bedrooms, and sitting rooms that surrounded it, to win general approval, she was much mistaken. As she later observed, it aroused "a concert of abuse".[2] The critics were all but unanimous in their contempt for it. *Art et Décoration*, which had admired her display in the 1913 Salon, termed this one laughable and abnormal. One critic described it as "a chamber for the daughter of Dr. Caligari in all its horrors".[3]

So odd did the room seem, however, that despite the fact that few admired it, photographs of it appeared in not only French but foreign journals. One of these brought a postcard from J. J. P. Oud, the leading architect of the Dutch de Stijl movement.

> Dear Miss Gray
>   In a Dutch review I saw a reproduction – a
> very bad one – of a room in Monte Carlo you designed.
> I am highly interested in it and should like to see
> any more of your works. Could you perhaps send me
> a number of a revue containing your works? I would
> be highly obliged by it as I saw until now very few
> good modern interiors.
>   I hope you will excuse my indiscretion.
>   Respectfully and sincerely
>   Yours
>   Oud
> Do you have any modern "movement" in your country?[4]

What the French found bizarre and ugly, the Dutch found exciting. Oud's endorsement must have come as a considerable reassurance to her. It is odd in one respect however: her work had already been "discovered" by other members of the de Stijl a year earlier.

In 1922, a large exhibition of French art from all periods had been sent to Amsterdam. It included a group of objects designed by Eileen Gray, and these were immediately noticed and admired by some of the de Stijl group, particularly Jan Wils, who subsequently entered into correspondence with her. Upset by the way her display was mounted, he obtained her permission to reinstall it more sympathetically.

This contact with Wils had a much more gratifying effect than his helping her with her exhibition, however. It led to the entire June 1924 issue of the influential Dutch art journal *Wendigen* being devoted to her work. Many of the illustrations are of the rue de Lota apartment, but there are as well views of the 1923 Salon, and of a number of individual pieces of furniture, lamps, screens, and carpets. It was a tribute she could be proud of.

By the time it was published, however, she was coming to see her own work in a new perspective. Not only Oud and Wils, but van Ravenstein, Walter Gropius, and Frederick Kiesler had shown interest in her. Undaunted by the reception her Monte Carlo room had received in the spring of 1923, she had exhibited again in the Salon d'Automne, along with Le Corbusier and Robert Mallet-Stevens, and had become friendly with them. She found herself taken up and encouraged by architects, and she was tempted to go beyond decoration and try architecture for herself.

NOTES
1. The term "art deco" was not coined until the 1960's, but is generally used to describe the style of decoration epitomized by the objects exhibited in the 1925 Paris *Exposition Internationale des Arts Décoratives et Industriels*. It is essentially conservative in form, achieving its effects by the use of rich materials and stylized surface decoration.
2. Antiquarius interview.
3. Unsigned article "*Le Salon des décorateurs*", an unidentified newspaper clipping, dated 5 May 1923, in the Eileen Gray papers.
4. The postcard was addressed to Enniscorthy, County Wexford, Ireland, and redirected to her Paris address. The article Oud read presumably, therefore, led him to believe that she lived in Ireland, which would explain his postcript.

Small table in oak and sycomore designed in 1922, the year she first met and corresponded with members of the Dutch de Stijl group. Its arrangement of cantilevered planes prefigures the massing that would characterize her architectural experiments later in the decade.

V E-1027 ROQUEBRUNE

E-1027 at Roquebrune: the west end, looking up from the suntrap.

In one of her chronologies, Eileen Gray noted that in 1924 she had begun making architectural studies. In time, daily coping with Jean Désert came to prove increasingly onorous, and she decided to concentrate, at least for a time, on her new interest. As she described it:

> I got to know Badovici, you see, and he said, "Why only furniture; it's perfectly absurd. Why don't you build"? And so I said, "That's all very well, as if I could build; I haven't had the requisite training". And he said, "But good heavens, you ought to cut off from all this and go down South and *learn*". I said, "You really think I could"? He said, "Yes, of course, and I shall be coming down". And then he did. I went down and found a place at St. Raphael that I could rent, and then I started really by myself sort of making plans of buildings.[1]

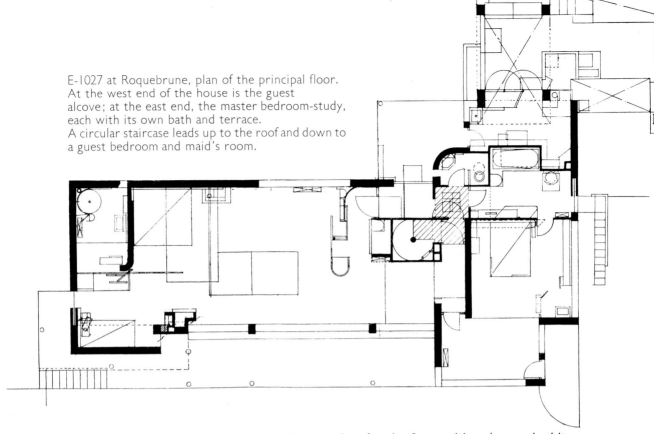

E-1027 at Roquebrune, plan of the principal floor.
At the west end of the house is the guest
alcove; at the east end, the master bedroom-study,
each with its own bath and terrace.
A circular staircase leads up to the roof and down to
a guest bedroom and maid's room.

Jean Badovici acted as the immediate catalyst for the first and best known building she would work on and in time became her collaborator in the project. He was a Romanian, trained as an architect, who had made a considerable reputation as an editor and writer on architectural themes, rather than as a designer of buildings. In fact, apart from his collaboration with Eileen Gray on their house at Roquebrune, he is known only to have built a later house for himself in Vézeley and a Paris house near the Pont de Sèvres. After the Second World War, he became interested in the development of a new, improved design for lifeboats. He died in 1956.

During the mid-1920s, Jean Badovici was the editor of l'*Architecture Vivante*, a journal that published the work of the leading avant-garde architects, and it was here that the house Eileen Gray and he designed appeared in a special number entitled *E-1027. Maison en Bord de Mer*. This contains full descriptive texts, numerous plans and drawings, and photographs of every aspect of the house and the furnishings that Eileen Gray designed for it.[2]

The house, which they named E-1027, was intended to advertise their ability and attract other jobs. The conception was of a retreat for a sportsman, an informal house, closely related to the sea below it, that could be opened up to the sun or closed down in bad weather. The centre of the house was a large livingroom in which the owner and guests could gather, but beyond this were numerous places affording privacy for each of the occupants.

E-1027 was planned with great care, and the result is exceptionally pleasing. The house seems casual, yet nothing is left to chance. It was much admired when it was built. Le Corbusier, who was a friend of Jean Badovici's, visited it often, in 1945, painting a large mural on one wall of the living room and eventually building a swimming cabin for himself on the rocks beneath it. It was from these rocks that he swam to his death.

E-1027 at Roquebrune from the sea. The house is approached from above, by a series of steps and paths leading down the steep, terraced hillside.

The "Transat" chair, designed by Eileen Gray in 1927. The padded leather seat is slung within the lacquer frame; the backrest pivots. The chromed steel connectors express the joints of the different parts of the frame.

The living room, the entire south wall of which can be opened by means of folding glass doors onto a terrace overlooking the sea.

The guest bedroom on the lower floor of E-1027 at Roquebrune. The circular table could be slid under the bed, the height of the top adjusted to make it possible to have breakfast in bed. The "6"-shaped structure hanging at the foot of the bed held mosquito netting.

Cantilevered table beside the divan in the guest alcove. It swings out of the way on two pivoting arms and has an adjustable easel to make it possible to read comfortably in bed. The stencilled legend on the cupboard, indicating the purpose of the storage area, is a device Eileen Gray used extensively throughout the house.

Guest alcove off the living room. The door leads to a small covered terrace on which a hammock could be hung. The cupboards at the head of the divan hold pillows, mosquito netting, books, a reading light, and tea things.

Built-in desk in guest room.

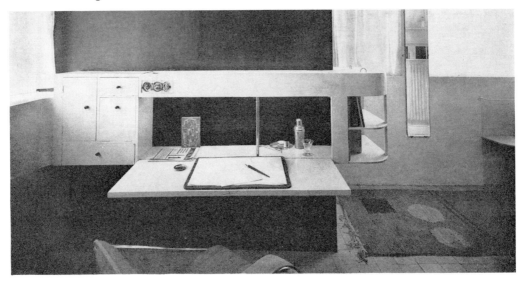

Lavatory at the end of the master bedroom. One section of the mirror above the basin turns to adjust the reflected image. The ingenious design for windows, which slide to one side on tracks, was patented by Jean Badovici in 1929.

Back of aluminium cupboard, which served to screen the lavatory from anyone entering the master bedroom.

Dressing cupboard, of aluminium and cork, seen at the right of the illustration on the preceding page. It faced into the master bedroom lavatory and when opened revealed drawers and shelves for toiletries and, on the inside of its door, a full-length mirror.

Suntrap on the terrace below the house, paved in glazed tiles and containing a built-in table. One section of its floor was inclined towards the south.

NOTES
1. Unidentified typescript, the transcription of a taped interview, in the Eileen Gray papers.
2. Several plates were printed in colour, but Eileen Gray noted in one of her scrapbooks that the pochoir colour was very inaccurate.

VI RUE CHATEAUBRIAND

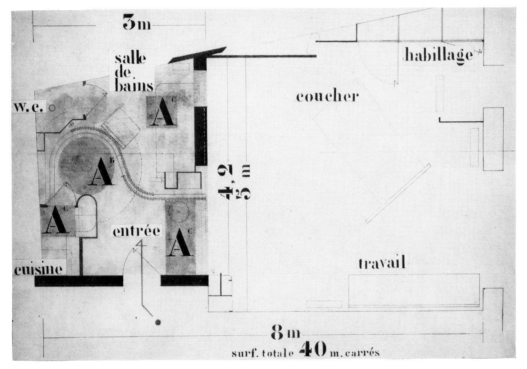

Plan of the Badovici apartment in the rue Châteaubriand. 'A' indicates storage area above the false ceiling, access to which was provided by folding ladders.

In 1930–31, Eileen Gray created a studio apartment for Jean Badovici out of a bare, irregularly shaped room 8 metres (26 feet) by approximately 5 metres (16 feet) in a building in the rue Châteaubriand, near the Champs Elysées. At one end she formed an entry, tiny kitchen, bar, and bathroom, the different parts of which could be thrown together or closed off by moving adjustable metal screens and curtains along curved tracks. Since the raw space was devoid of storage accommodation, she built a false ceiling over this service area, with four storage compartments above.

One wall of the room was angled, and in the larger, living area she brought this forward, making a new square room, to each portion of which she assigned a specific function. Along the wall running back from the larger of two windows, she placed a long work table, with a cork board and strip work light above. In front of the second, smaller window, she created a dressing alcove by placing a tall mirror at right angles to

Inner end of the room, looking towards the entry. The section of dropped ceiling containing three flush lights, swings down to reveal one of the storage spaces.

The window wall, behind which were large cupboards. In front of it is the dressing alcove. The work table and light on the opposite side of the room is seen in reflection.

the window and an aluminium-backed cabinet in front of it. It was a variation of the aluminium-and-cork cupboard she had made for her own bedroom at Roquebrune and served, as that one had, to provide handy storage, to separate spaces intended for different uses, and to give an unexpected, strong visual accent to the room.

The new storage wall she constructed on this side of the room was faced with floor-to-ceiling mirrors, which both gave the illusion of added space and further reflected the dressing area. In the centre of the room, on a diagonal, she built a divan (complete with reading light and pivoting table surface), and before it she set one of her adjustable round tables. In the corner near the service area was a small dining table, flanked by a tubular metal chair and a leather hassock (which being between the table and the divan could relate equally well to either). On the other side of the room, near the work table, was a Transat chair; and finally, in the middle of the back wall, was a four-panel screen made not of lacquer but of painted industrial grating set within a narrow wooden frame.

The new apartment, despite its small size, provided for the varied needs of its user with ingenuity and sophistication. Also, and more importantly, despite the rational functional programme set down and worked within by the designer, her sensitive use of textures (metal, mirrors, textiles, furs) and the care with which she treated details, prevented it from seeming in any way cold, schematic or doctrinaire – the qualities attributed to so many contemporary modernist interiors by their critics.

Entry to the one-room apartment Eileen Gray designed for Jean Badovici, divided into a small kitchen, bar, and bathroom by aluminium and wood panels and by a heavy metallic curtain that moved on a curved track. The dropped ceiling concealed storage space for valises, papers, and household equipment.

VII   TEMPE A PAILLA, CASTELLAR

Between 1932 and 1934, Eileen Gray designed and built for herself a second small house. The site she chose was at least as restricting as had been that at Roquebrune. It lay 4 kilometres from Menton on a precipitous, terraced hill. The narrow strip of ground available for construction was sandwiched between a public road and a passage leading to another house; the land available to her for a garden was on the other side of the passage, separate from the house site. The spot recommended itself to her, however, because of its spectacular views, which embraced both sea and mountains, looking out over the valley and towards the Italian frontier.

Another recommendation was the fact that the site contained three cisterns, which she would be able to incorporate in the house. Building on this base, she used one as a garage, another as a storage cellar, and the third to hold water collected on the flat roof of the house.

The house itself is built of reinforced concrete above a rough stone pedestal. Access to the garden is by means of a bridge that spans the passage; and despite the fact that the house is hemmed in on both sides, the effect from inside is of being moored in air at treetop level rather than on the ground itself.

On the main floor is a large living terrace, the largest space in the house, behind which is a studio-living room, dining room, kitchen, bath, master bedroom and a small second bedroom. Below the living terrace, because of the fall of the land, there is room for a mezzanine containing a guest bedroom and bath and below that a garage.

Eileen Gray lived in Tempe a Pailla until the Second World War. In 1939 she arranged and furnished a small flat for herself in St. Tropez, but it was destroyed in 1944 and no record of it survives. In 1940 she was exiled as an enemy alien to Lourmarin in the Vaucluse, and on her return to Castellar after the war she discovered that little but its walls remained. It had been occupied successively by Italian, German and American troops and had been looted.

She began to rebuild the house and remake the furniture; but by 1956 her eyesight had deteriorated to the point where she was no longer able to drive. She decided, therefore, to retire to her old Paris apartment in the rue Bonaparte, and sold Tempe a Pailla to the English painter Graham Sutherland.

The entrance to Tempe a Pailla from the road. The garage is built in what had been an old cistern. Steps beyond the gate lead upward to the guestroom level and continue to the living terrace.

Throughout the house sliding windows and shutters set in tracks
are used for privacy and protection from the glare of the sun.

The house from the road below. Stretching to the left of the living terrace is the bridge over the passage, giving access to the garden.

Overleaf: The living terrace. Here, too, sliding shutters within tracks are used to open up or shield the space. Through the opening in the wall on the right can be glimpsed the public road. The glass wall to the rear leads into studio-living room.

Detail of the window louvres, showing the handle with which they are adjusted.

The work area of the studio-living room. The louvres in front of the strip of windows high in the wall pivot to regulate the intensity of light permitted to enter.

The living end of the studio-living room. Behind the rectangle above the radiator is the strip of windows seen in the illustration showing the exterior from the road.

Metal wardrobe in the master bedroom.
It moves on tracks and can be opened by pulling it laterally.

Small chest, closed, with two tiers of drawers, each of which pivots. Eileen Gray used pivoting drawers in different combinations repeatedly in her work from at least 1923. This chest, however, is her most fully realized treatment of the motif. Joe Colombo's 1968 design for the "Boby" stand bears a marked, and perhaps not entirely coincidental resemblance to it, since the Gray design was published in Roberto Aloi's influential *L'Arredamento Moderno* (second series) in 1939.

Pivoting chest, open.

The dining room, seen from the entrance to the studio-living room. The built-in couch, when drawn forward, reveals a narrow staircase leading down into the storage cellar in what had previously been one of the cisterns. The table on its slotted metal base, can be wheeled forward or back.

VIII PROJECTS

Many of the ideas Eileen Gray was unable to build, she nonetheless worked through with plans, technical drawings, and elaborate models. She had begun making architectural studies in 1924, and through the rest of her long life she returned to them. The earliest of which any record survives is a 1926 project for a house for an engineer to be built in the Midi. Constructed on pilotis, as was E-1027, it is a much simpler structure than the house she and Jean Badovici decided instead to build in that year.

In 1933 she designed a house and studio for two sculptors, and in 1937 an elliptical "tube" house. By now, however, her interests had considerably broadened, and she worked out a complex scheme for a vacation centre, including offices, garages, demountable cabins, a large youth hostel, a restaurant, gymnasium, and a theatre. Le Corbusier was much taken with it and drawings and the maquettes for the various elements were exhibited in his pavilion at the 1937 Paris International Exposition.

Her last major project, on which she worked from 1946 to 1949, during the time she was attempting to rebuild her war-damaged house at Castellar, was for a cultural and social centre, which included conference rooms, galleries, a library, theatre, restaurant, and outdoor theatre.

Once Eileen Gray returned to Paris, she went into virtual retirement. She had an operation on one eye, but her sight did not improve. She did still work intermittently on her projects and attempted to find ways to incorporate the new materials that had reached the market since the War into furniture. In her mid-80s she converted an old barn near St. Tropez for her use as a summer house. It was her last building, but it was not to be the end of her career.

When Eileen Gray was in her nineties, a younger generation of designers, architects, and, by now, historians, began to take a fresh interest in her work and to seek her out. Although essentially shy, she responded to their interest, showing them her work and, with their encouragement, putting some of her most original designs – which had been too advanced for general acceptance when conceived – into production. Shortly before she died in 1976 at the age of 97, she was even able to see her work featured in the exhibition "1925" at the Museé des Arts Décoratifs in Paris.

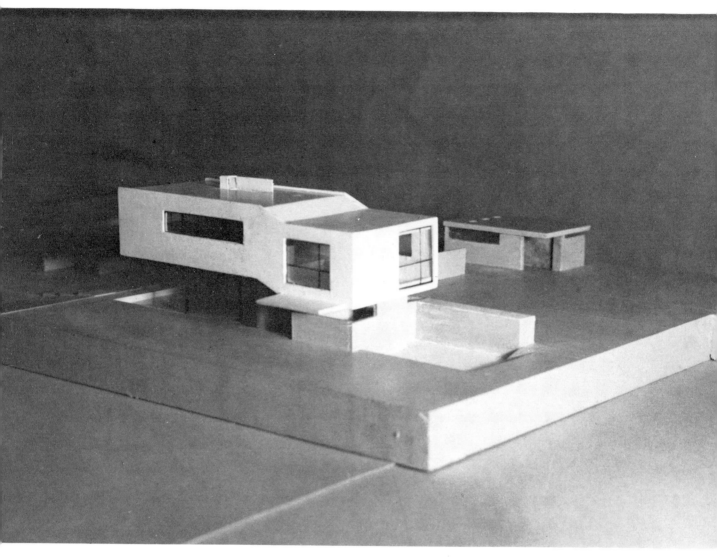

ENGINEER'S HOUSE
This project was developed in the same year Eileen Gray began work on E-1027 at Roquebrune.

HOUSE FOR TWO SCULPTORS
One section of the wall of the egg-shaped studio folds back, allowing massive pieces of sculpture to be moved in and out.

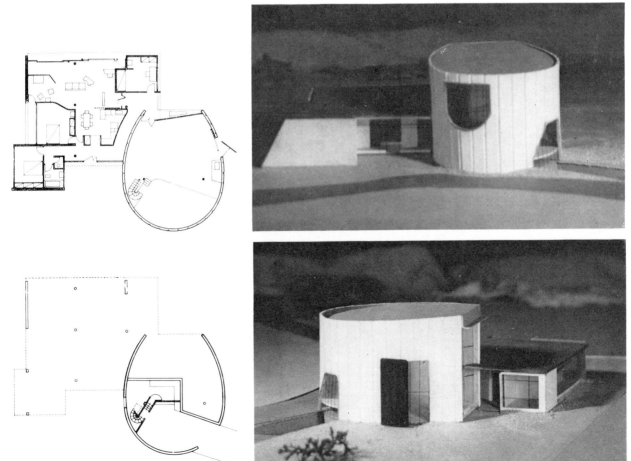

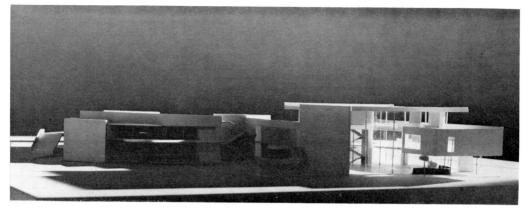

CULTURAL AND SOCIAL CENTRE
Eileen Gray's last architectural project provided for a multiplicity of activities within a single structure. Its most striking feature was the sloped roof over the cinema-theatre, which in turn provided seating for the open-air theatre above.

TUBE HOUSE
These small units were intended to be capable of being prefabricated and set up, either singly or in series, in the shortest possible time and with a minimum of foundation. They could serve either as summer camps or as emergency housing. Each unit contained two bedrooms, a living area-kitchen, and toilet.

VACATION CENTRE
The plan indicates the many activities provided for in the scheme, which was exhibited by Le Corbusier in the 1937 Paris Exposition Internationale.

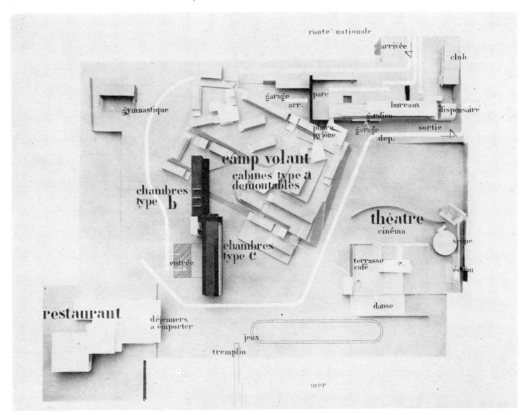

IX CONCLUSION

Looked at in one light, Eileen Gray's career breaks neatly in half. There seems to be very little connection between the luxurious, meticulously finished objects that preceded 1923 and the rigorously intellectualized work that followed it. Scholars and collectors drawn to one period tend to ignore the other; they seem to have so little relevance to each other.

And yet, despite the dissimilarities between early and late styles, there is an overriding consistency about her work and her life. Themes recur: the manipulation of pivoting drawers, for example, the fascination with barriers that at once define space and are penetrated by it. Many of the ideas developed in her late work are implicit in the early. Her career, seen as a whole, is one of ever broadening horizons, of a lively intelligence and genuine talent constantly exploring, testing, and moving on, never satisfied, always on the go.

To understand her, one must have some appreciation of the world that shaped her, however hard she may have attempted to shape it. Born into a privileged, provincial society, she broke away early, initially taking the relatively safe and conventional path of art school in London but almost immediately – and entirely characteristically – moving off on her own, to work in an extraordinarily demanding medium. There were plenty of young women in London at the turn of the century, the height of the arts-and-crafts craze, creating hand-made objects, but it seems safe to say that she was the only one with the imagination and courage to tackle oriental lacquer.

Once she had mastered her craft, she began to investigate new ways to use it, working always within the framework of her own vision, never within the confines of popular taste. Had she been born fifty years later she probably would have trained as an architect, but it was only chance that brought her to the attention of Jan Wils, Oud, and the other de Stijl architects. Without their encouragement and that of Jan Badovici, Christian Zervos, and Le Corbusier, she might never have attempted architecture. But once she had tried building – had, in a sense, gotten her hands on space – there was no going back.

Her architectural output was negligible – two houses, both for herself, an apartment, some projects, ambitious but unrealized. But it must be remembered that she was a woman working almost entirely alone on the edge of a profession that was both highly organized and almost exclusively male.

There were two other women in the period whose talents and achievements may be compared with Eileen Gray's: Lilly Reich and Charlotte Perriand. Both of them, however, worked in close proximity to and remained much in the shadow of the men with whom they worked – Reich with Mies van der Rohe and Perriand with Le Corbusier. But Eileen Gray did not find it easy either to collaborate or to share. Although she and Jean Badovici remained friends, they worked as partners only once. And it is significant that instead of choosing (or being chosen by) a towering figure such as Mies or Le Corbusier, she found someone she could lead. The billing for E-1027 at Roquebrune is "Eileen Gray and Jean Badovici", not the other way round.

Ultimately she was most comfortable alone, working out her own ideas, solving her problems her own way. Her work had little influence on her contemporaries; only E-1027 at Roquebrune, thanks to Badovici and l'Architecture Vivante, was widely known. And yet her designs, both early and late speak to us with freshness, intelligence, and integrity. She was, first and last, an original.